BOOK 2

Ruth Miskin

Superphonics

The simplest, fastest way to
teach your child to read

Contents

Hodder
Children's
Books

a division of Hodder Headline

D0230933

Introduction

What is meant by the term 'phonics'?

Phonics is a highly effective way of teaching reading and spelling, based on the link between sounds and the way in which we write them down. A unit of sound is called a phoneme (*foe-neem*), and the written version of it is called a grapheme:

c / a / t   contains 3 graphemes and 3 phonemes

ch / a / t   contains 3 graphemes and 3 phonemes

f / l / a / t contains 4 graphemes and 4 phonemes

Note: A phoneme may contain more than one letter. A letter has a name: *dee*
and a sound: *d (d)*

Letters are divided into 2 groups:
Vowels: *a e i o u*
Consonants: *b c d f g h j k l m n p q r s t v w x y z*

How does *Superphonics* teach this?

There are 5 books in the series. The chart on the inside front cover shows which graphemes/ phonemes are taught in each book. Each book builds on the skills already learned, and there are plenty of opportunities for revision and practice.

Each book is divided into units, all of which are organised in the same way.

Each unit in this book and Books 3–5 consists of 6 steps:

STEP 1 FIND THE RHYMING WORDS
The ability to rhyme is an important skill. If your child can read and spell *cat*, he or she will be able to read and spell *mat* – and so on.

STEP 2 FIND THE SOUNDS
Now your child is taught to hear the separate phonemes in a word: *c / a / t*. Most children need to be taught that each word is made up of individual sounds. This comes in Book 3.

STEP 3 BLEND THE SOUNDS
The little alien Phoneme Fred is useful here. Poor Phoneme Fred can only speak in separate phonemes – *c / a / t* – and your child will be able to help him to blend these into a spoken word.

STEP 4 SPLIT THE WORD INTO SOUNDS
Hearing the phonemes, and saying them in quick succession, prepares children for spelling.

STEP 5 READ THE WORD
Your child is taught how to read the word phoneme by phoneme, always going from left to right.

STEP 6 SPELL THE WORD
This is a writing activity, in which your child will learn how to turn the phonemes into graphemes, or written letters. Ask your child to read his or her writing back to you.

   Some children take time to learn how to write. Don't spend too long on this step, and don't worry if your child's spelling is not developing as quickly as his or her reading.

Phoneme Fred

This is a double-page spread from Book 2.

This text tells you what to do.

This text is 'script' for you to read aloud to your child.

This text is for your child to read. A few words are printed in blue. These are difficult words, or words which contain graphemes which have not yet been taught. You may need to help your child to read these.

Helpful hints are printed in boxes like this.

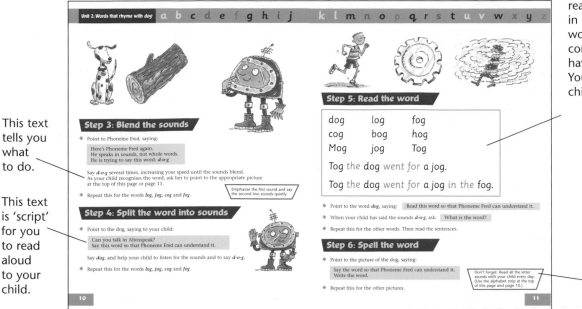

How do I know it will work?

In the author's school, where this method is used, the reading ages of children in Years 2 to 4 are about 2 years higher than their actual ages.

I'm not a teacher – will I be able to do it?

Yes! *Superphonics* is clearly structured and clearly written, in plain English. The 'step' method of working will rapidly become familiar to you and your child.

My life is very busy – how much time will it take up?

If you spend just 20 minutes on *Superphonics* each day, your child will make swift progress. Book 1 will take about 4 weeks, Book 2 will take 2-6 weeks and Books 3-5 will each take 1-2 weeks to complete. If you can't manage 20 minutes every day, don't worry. Just do what you can.

Will I need to collect lots of bits and pieces before we can start?

No! All you need, apart from the books, is a notebook or a few sheets of paper, and a sharp pencil. A small mirror (for looking at mouth shape) is useful but not essential.

Will *Superphonics* enable my child to read stories?

Yes! He or she will be able to read stories, street signs, lists, adverts – and lots more! But don't wait until you have finished *Superphonics* to share books and other kinds of reading.

This book teaches 3-letter words such as *cat, hen, pig, dog* and *bug*. Your child will learn to listen for the first sound, the last sound and the middle sound (the most difficult). The middle sounds (vowels) are taught in order of difficulty: *a o e u i*.

At this stage, it is best to refer to a letter by its sound (*d*) rather than its name (*dee*).

Step 1: Find the rhyming words

◆ Look at the big picture together.
Say:

> Can you see Pat the cat?
> Pat wants to hear some words that sound like her name.

◆ Ask your child to find things in the picture whose names sound like *cat*, and say the words together:

> **mat hat rat sat fat bat**

Sat is a verb (a word that describes an action), and *fat* is an adjective (a describing word). Encourage your child to use these words as well as the nouns (naming words): *The fat cat sat on the mat.*

◆ Help your child to think of more words that rhyme with *cat*, and say the words together, for example:

> **that flat chat at gnat**

Say each word very clearly. Make your mouth as round as an apple as you say *a*. Let your child do this, looking at the shape of his mouth in a mirror.

◆ Make up some nonsense words to rhyme with *cat*, for example:

> **lat dat blat**

◆ Make up some rhyming sentences or phrases such as:

> The cat sat on the rat with a hat.
> The cat sat on a flat hat.
> Splat! The cat sat on the rat.

Repeat these together, exaggerating the *a* sound, until your child can say them quickly.

Step 2: Find the sounds

◆ Point to the cat, saying:

> What sound can you hear at the beginning of *cat*?
> Listen: *c c cat*
>
> What sound can you hear at the end of *cat*?
>
> What sound can you hear in the middle of *cat*?

Use the sound of the letter rather than its name. Make the sound very short (*c*, not *cuh*).

Exaggerate the *t* sound as you say *cat*.

The middle sound (*a*) is the hardest to hear. Make your mouth as round as an apple as you say *cat*.

◆ Repeat this for words that rhyme with *cat*.

Step 3: Blend the sounds

◆ Point to Phoneme Fred, saying:

> This is Phoneme Fred.
> He speaks in sounds, not whole words.
> He is trying to say this word: *c-a-t*

Say *c-a-t* several times, increasing your speed until the sounds blend.
As your child recognises the word, ask him to point to the appropriate picture
at the top of this page or page 7.

◆ Repeat this for the words *mat, rat, hat* and *bat*.

> Emphasise the first sound and say
> the second two sounds quietly.

Step 4: Split the word into sounds

◆ Point to the cat, saying to your child:

> Can you talk in Alienspeak?
> Say this word so that Phoneme Fred can understand it.

Say *cat*, and help your child to listen for the sounds and to say *c-a-t*.

◆ Repeat this for the words *mat, rat, hat* and *bat*.

> You may need to demonstrate
> this a few times.

Step 5: Read the word

cat   sat   hat

Pat   fat   <u>ch</u>at

rat   bat   mat

A cat sat on a mat.

<u>Th</u>at fat cat in a hat sat on a mat.

> Point to each letter in turn, emphasising the left-to-right movement.

> Words containing graphemes which have not yet been taught are printed in blue.

> Your child should say the sounds increasingly quickly until they blend to make the word.

◆ Point to the word *cat*, saying: Read this word so that Phoneme Fred can understand it.

◆ When your child has said the sounds *c-a-t*, ask: What is the word?

◆ Repeat this for the other words. Then read the sentences.

Step 6: Spell the word

> You may need to help your child to write the words.

◆ Point to the picture of the cat, saying:

Say the word so that Phoneme Fred can understand it.
Write the word.

> Don't forget: Read all the letter sounds with your child every day. (Use the alphabet strip at the top of this page and page 6.)

◆ Repeat this for the other pictures.

Unit 2: Words that rhyme with *dog*

Step 1: Find the rhyming words

◆ Look at the big picture together.
Say:

> Can you see Tog the dog?
> Tog wants to hear some words that sound like her name.

◆ Ask your child to find things in the picture whose names sound like *dog*, and say the words together:

> *cog fog jog log*

Jog is a verb (a word that describes an action).

◆ Help your child to think of more words that rhyme with *dog*, and say the words together, for example:

> *bog hog*

Say each word very clearly. Shape your lips like an *o* as you say the *o* sound. Let your child do this, looking at her mouth in a mirror.

◆ Make up some nonsense words to rhyme with *dog*, for example:

> *nog rog sog zog*

◆ Make up some rhyming sentences or phrases such as:

> Tog the dog got lost in the fog.
> Jog with a dog in the fog.

Encourage your child to make up her own words and rhymes.

Repeat these together, exaggerating the *o* sound, until your child can say them quickly.

Step 2: Find the sounds

◆ Point to the dog, saying:

> What sound can you hear at the beginning of *dog*?
> Listen: *d d dog*
>
> What sound can you hear at the end of *dog*?
>
> What sound can you hear in the middle of *dog*?

Use the sound of the letter rather than its name. Make the sound very short (*d*, not *duh*).

Exaggerate the *g* sound as you say *dog*.

The middle sound (*o*) is the hardest to hear. Shape your lips like an *o* as you say *dog*.

◆ Repeat this for words that rhyme with *dog*.

f g h i j k l m n o p q r s t u v w x y z

Step 3: Blend the sounds

◆ Point to Phoneme Fred, saying:

> Here's Phoneme Fred again.
> He speaks in sounds, not whole words.
> He is trying to say this word: *d-o-g*

Say *d-o-g* several times, increasing your speed until the sounds blend.
As your child recognises the word, ask her to point to the appropriate picture
at the top of this page or page 11.

◆ Repeat this for the words *log*, *jog*, *cog* and *fog*.

> Emphasise the first sound and say
> the second two sounds quietly.

Step 4: Split the word into sounds

◆ Point to the dog, saying to your child:

> Can you talk in Alienspeak?
> Say this word so that Phoneme Fred can understand it.

Say *dog*, and help your child to listen for the sounds and to say *d-o-g*.

◆ Repeat this for the words *log*, *jog*, *cog* and *fog*.

Step 5: Read the word

dog log fog

cog bog hog

Mog jog Tog

Tog the **dog** went for a jog.

Tog the **dog** went for a jog in the **fog**.

◆ Point to the word *dog*, saying: Read this word so that Phoneme Fred can understand it.

◆ When your child has said the sounds *d-o-g*, ask: What is the word?

◆ Repeat this for the other words. Then read the sentences.

Step 6: Spell the word

◆ Point to the picture of the dog, saying:

> Say the word so that Phoneme Fred can understand it.
> Write the word.

Don't forget: Read all the letter sounds with your child every day. (Use the alphabet strip at the top of this page and page 10.)

◆ Repeat this for the other pictures.

Words that rhyme with *cat* and *dog*

◆ Ask your child to read Pat the cat's words and Tog the dog's words, emphasising the middle vowel sound (***a*** or ***o***).

cat
hat
fat
pat
mat
sat
rat

dog
bog
fog
log
hog
jog
cog

- Tell your child that Pat the cat's words have been mixed up with Tog the dog's words. They are not very pleased!

- Ask your child to read each word, and to tell you which animal it belongs to.

cat   dog   fog

sat   jog   mat

log   fat   hat

cog   bog   rat

Unit 3: Words that rhyme with *hen*

Step 1: Find the rhyming words

◆ Look at the big picture together.
   Say:

> Can you see Jen the hen?
> Jen wants to hear some words that sound like her name.

◆ Ask your child to find things in the picture whose names sound like **hen**, and say the words together:

> **men ten den pen**

◆ Help your child to think of more words that rhyme with **hen**, and say the words together, for example:

> **Ben Ken then when fen wren**

> Say each word very clearly. Pretend you are eating a spoonful of egg as you say **e**. Let your child do this, looking at the shape of his mouth in a mirror.

◆ Make up some nonsense words to rhyme with **hen**, for example:

> **nen sen ven**

◆ Make up some rhyming sentences or phrases such as:

> Ten men in a pen with Jen

Repeat these together, exaggerating the *e* sound, until your child can say them quickly.

Step 2: Find the sounds

◆ Point to the hen, saying:

> What sound can you hear at the beginning of **hen**?
> Listen: **h h hen**
>
> What sound can you hear at the end of **hen**?
>
> What sound can you hear in the middle of **hen**?

> Use the sound of the letter rather than its name.
> Make the sound very short (**h**, not **huh**).

> Exaggerate the *n* sound as you say **hen**.

> The middle sound (*e*) is the hardest to hear. Pretend to be eating a spoonful of egg as you say **hen**.

◆ Repeat this for words that rhyme with **hen**.

Step 3: Blend the sounds

◆ Point to Phoneme Fred, saying:

> Here's Phoneme Fred again.
> He speaks in sounds, not whole words.
> He is trying to say this word: **_h-e-n_**

Say **_h-e-n_** several times, increasing your speed until the sounds blend.
As your child recognises the word, ask him to point to the appropriate picture
at the top of this page or page 17.

◆ Repeat this for the words **_men, pen, ten_** and **_den_**.

> Emphasise the first sound and say
> the second two sounds quietly.

Step 4: Split the word into sounds

◆ Point to the hen, saying to your child:

> Can you talk in Alienspeak?
> Say this word so that Phoneme Fred can understand it.

Say **_hen_**, and help your child to listen for the sounds and to say **_h-e-n_**.

◆ Repeat this for the words **_men, pen, ten_** and **_den_**.

Step 5: Read the word

hen   ten   pen ˅

men   den   <u>th</u>en

fen   Jen   Ben

Ken and Ben in a pen with a hen

Ten men in a pen with a hen

◆ Point to the word **hen,** saying: Read this word so that Phoneme Fred can understand it.

◆ When your child has said the sounds **h-e-n**, ask: What is the word?

◆ Repeat this for the other words. Then read the phrases.

Step 6: Spell the word

◆ Point to the picture of the hen, saying:

Say the word so that Phoneme Fred can understand it.
Write the word.

◆ Repeat this for the other pictures.

> Don't forget: Read all the letter sounds with your child every day. (Use the alphabet strip at the top of this page and page 16.)

Words that rhyme with *cat*, *dog* and *hen*

◆ Ask your child to read Pat the cat's words, Tog the dog's words and Jen the hen's words, emphasising the middle vowel sound (*a, o* or *e*).

cat	dog	hen
bat	bog	ten
sat	fog	men
hat	log	<u>th</u>en
mat	hog	den
fat	jog	fen
rat	cog	pen

- Tell your child that Pat the cat's words have been mixed up with Tog the dog's words and Jen the hen's words. They are not very pleased!

- Ask your child to read each word, and to tell you which animal it belongs to.

dog	pen	hen
men	fog	cat
log	mat	jog
sat	ten	rat

Step 1: Find the rhyming words

◆ Look at the big picture together.
Say:

> Can you see Zug the bug?
> Zug wants to hear some words that sound like her name.

◆ Ask your child to find things in the picture whose names sound like *bug*, and say the words together:

> *rug hug jug mug slug plug*

Say each word very clearly. Tell your child that **Zug** the *bug* has lost his umbrella and is saying: *Where is my u u umbrella?*

◆ Help your child to think of more words that rhyme with *bug*, and say the words together, for example:

> *chug dug tug snug pug shrug*

◆ Make up some nonsense words to rhyme with *bug*, for example:

> *spug nug sug*

◆ Make up some rhyming sentences or phrases such as:

> The slug dug up a snug bug.
> As snug as a bug in a rug

Repeat these together, exaggerating the *u* sound, until your child can say them quickly.

Step 2: Find the sounds

◆ Point to the bug, saying:

> What sound can you hear at the beginning of *bug*?
> Listen: *b b bug*
>
> What sound can you hear at the end of *bug*?
>
> What sound can you hear in the middle of *bug*?

Use the sound of the letter rather than its name. Make the sound very short (*b*, not *buh*).

Exaggerate the *g* sound as you say *bug*.

The middle sound (*u*) is the hardest to hear.

◆ Repeat this for words that rhyme with *bug*.

Step 3: Blend the sounds

◆ Point to Phoneme Fred, saying:

> Here's Phoneme Fred again.
> He speaks in sounds, not whole words.
> He is trying to say this word: *b-u-g*

Say *b-u-g* several times, increasing your speed until the sounds blend.
As your child recognises the word, ask her to point to the appropriate picture
at the top of this page or page 23.

> Emphasise the first sound and say
> the second two sounds quietly.

◆ Repeat this for the words *rug*, *mug*, *jug* and *hug*.

Step 4: Split the word into sounds

◆ Point to the bug, saying to your child:

> Can you talk in Alienspeak?
> Say this word so that Phoneme Fred can understand it.

Say *bug*, and help your child to listen for the sounds and to say *b-u-g*.

◆ Repeat this for the words *rug*, *mug*, *jug* and *hug*.

Step 5: Read the word

bug	hug	rug
mug	dug	<u>ch</u>ug
pug	jug	tug

A bug on a mug and a bug on a jug

A mug and a jug with a bug and a rug

◆ Point to the word **bug,** saying: Read this word so that Phoneme Fred can understand it.

◆ When your child has said the sounds **b-u-g**, ask: What is the word?

◆ Repeat this for the other words. Then read the phrases.

Step 6: Spell the word

◆ Point to the picture of the bug, saying:

Say the word so that Phoneme Fred can understand it.
Write the word.

Don't forget: Read all the letter sounds with your child every day. (Use the alphabet strip at the top of this page and page 22.)

◆ Repeat this for the other pictures.

Words that rhyme with *cat*, *dog*, *hen* and *bug*

◆ Ask your child to read Pat the cat's words, Tog the dog's words, Jen the hen's words and Zug the bug's words, emphasising the middle vowel sound (*a*, *o*, *e* or *u*).

fat	fog	ten	rug
bat	jog	<u>th</u>en	bug
rat	hog	den	jug
hat	dog	men	tug
sat	bog	pen	hug
cat	log	hen	mug
mat	cog	fen	pug

♦ Tell your child that Pat the cat's words have been mixed up with Tog the dog's words, Jen the hen's words and Zug the bug's words. They are not very pleased!

♦ Ask your child to read each word, and to tell you which animal it belongs to.

cat   dog   hen

mug   rug   sat

men   ten   fog

log   bug   hat

Step 1: Find the rhyming words

◆ Look at the big picture together.
Say:

> Can you see Mig the pig?
> Mig wants to hear some words that sound like her name.

◆ Ask your child to find things in the picture whose names sound like *pig*, and say the words together:

> *big fig jig wig twig*

Big is an adjective (a describing word). Encourage your child to use this word as well as the nouns (naming words):
The big pig has a big fig.

◆ Help your child to think of more words that rhyme with *pig*, and say the words together, for example:

> *dig gig rig swig sprig*

Say each word very clearly.

◆ Make up some nonsense words to rhyme with *pig*, for example:

> *kig hig chig*

◆ Make up some rhyming sentences or phrases such as:

> Jig in a wig, little pig.
> Dig with a twig, little pig.

Repeat these together, exaggerating the *i* sound, until your child can say them quickly.

Step 2: Find the sounds

◆ Point to the pig, saying:

> What sound can you hear at the beginning of *pig*?
> Listen: *p p pig*
>
> What sound can you hear at the end of *pig*?
>
> What sound can you hear in the middle of *pig*?

Always use the sound of the letter rather than its name. Make the sound very short (*p*, not *puh*).

Exaggerate the *g* sound as you say *pig*.

◆ Repeat this for words that rhyme with *pig*.

The middle sound (*i*) is the hardest to hear.

Step 3: Blend the sounds

◆ Point to Phoneme Fred, saying:

> Here's Phoneme Fred again.
> He speaks in sounds, not whole words.
> He is trying to say this word: ***p-i-g***

Say ***p-i-g*** several times, increasing your speed until the sounds blend.
As your child recognises the word, ask him to point to the appropriate picture
at the top of this page or page 29.

◆ Repeat this for the words ***wig, twig, jig*** and ***fig***.

> Emphasise the first sound and say
> the second two sounds quietly.

Step 4: Split the word into sounds

◆ Point to the pig, saying to your child:

> Can you talk in Alienspeak?
> Say this word so that Phoneme Fred can understand it.

Say ***pig***, and help your child to listen for the sounds and to say ***p-i-g***.

◆ Repeat this for the words ***wig, twig, jig*** and ***fig***.

Step 5: Read the word

pig	dig	fig
jig	wig	rig
Mig	big	gig

A big pig

A pig in a wig

◆ Point to the word *pig*, saying: Read this word so that Phoneme Fred can understand it.

◆ When your child has said the sounds *p-i-g*, ask: What is the word?

◆ Repeat this for the other words. Then read the phrases.

Step 6: Spell the word

◆ Point to the picture of the pig, saying:

Say the word so that Phoneme Fred can understand it.
Write the word.

Don't forget: Read all the letter sounds with your child every day. (Use the alphabet strip at the top of this page and page 28.)

◆ Repeat this for the other pictures.

Words that rhyme with *cat*, *dog*, *hen*, *bug* and *pig*

◆ Ask your child to read Pat the cat's words, Tog the dog's words, Jen the hen's words, Zug the bug's words and Mig the pig's words, emphasising the middle vowel sound (*a, o, e, u* or *i*).

cat	dog	hen	bug	pig
mat	log	<u>th</u>en	dug	wig
sat	fog	ten	hug	big
<u>th</u>at	jog	pen	jug	jig
rat	cog	men	mug	gig
bat	bog	fen	rug	dig
fat	hog	den	tug	fig

◆ Tell your child that Pat the cat's words have been mixed up with Tog the dog's words,
Jen the hen's words, Zug the bug's words and Mig the pig's words. They are not very pleased!

◆ Ask your child to read each word, and to tell you which animal it belongs to.

cat   pig   hen

bug   dog   pen

log   rug   big

fog   ten   wig

mug   mat   sat

◆ Read these questions and answers with your child.

He or she should be familiar with most of the words by now, but the pictures give plenty of clues!

A pig in a pen, a hen on a log, a dog in a hat, a cat on a rug and a bug in a wig?   No

A pig on a log, a hen in a hat, a dog on a rug, a cat in a wig and a bug in a pen?   No

A pig in a hat, a hen on a rug, a dog in a wig, a cat in a pen and a bug on a log?   No

A pig in a wig, a hen in a pen, a dog on a log, a cat in a hat and a bug on a rug?   Yes

Well done!
You have finished *Superphonics Book 2*, and you are now ready to start *Book 3* !

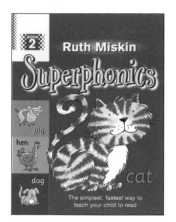

ISBN 0 340 77345 6 (paperback)
0 340 78768 6 (hardback)

ISBN 0 340 77346 4

ISBN 0 340 77347 2

ISBN 0 340 77348 0

ISBN 0 340 77349 9

Superphonics books are available from all good bookshops. They can also be ordered with a credit card direct from the publisher on 01235 400414.

ISBN 0 340 77346 4

Text © Ruth Miskin 2000
Illustrations © Kate Sheppard 2000

Editorial by Gill Munton
Design by Fiona Webb

The rights of Ruth Miskin and Kate Sheppard to be identified as the author and illustrator of this work have been asserted by them in accordance with the Copyright, Design and Patents Act 1988.

First published in Great Britain 2000

10 9 8 7 6 5 4 3 2 1

Published by Hodder Children's Books, a division of Hodder Headline plc, 338 Euston Road, London NW1 3BH

Printed in Hong Kong

A CIP record is registered by and held at the British Library.

Superphonics is a highly effective and enjoyable way to teach your child to read at home. It is based on the phonics approach widely used in schools. Phonics shows children the connection between letters and sounds, giving them the tools they need to read and spell with confidence.

bug

RUTH MISKIN is a head teacher and a leading authority on phonics. She provides Literacy training to schools across the country. **SUPERPHONICS** is based on the method she has evolved to teach reading and spelling to children at her own primary school, with remarkable success.

pig

BOOK 2 **T**his book shows you how to introduce your child to three-letter words. By the end of the book, he or she will be able to read – and spell – words such as **cat**, **dog** and **bug**.

hen

dog

Early Learning Goals

SUPERPHONICS helps your child build key skills in line with the new Early Learning Goals for preschool children.

Hodder Children's Books

ISBN 0-340-77346-4
00499

£4.99   9 780340 773468

cover illustration: Kate Sheppard